# Wood-Carving for Amateurs.

## A PRACTICAL HANDBOOK FOR THE NOVICE WORKER.

### *ILLUSTRATED.*

By  DAVID  DENNING,

*Author of " Fretwork and Marqueterie." &c.*

*FOURTH EDITION.*

Revised and Enlarged by CHARLES F. CALLOW, A.R.I.B.A.

# CONTENTS.

| CHAP. | | PAGE |
|---|---|---|
| I.—Preliminary .. .. .. .. .. .. .. .. .. | | 1 |
| II.—Tools .. .. .. .. .. .. .. .. .. .. .. | | 5 |
| III.—Wood .. .. .. .. .. .. .. .. .. .. | | 14 |
| IV.—Bench, and Methods of Holding Work | .. | 19 |
| V.—Sharpening Tools .. .. .. .. .. .. .. | | 28 |
| VI.—Panel Carving .. .. .. .. .. .. .. | | 34 |
| VII.—Various Examples for Carving .. .. .. | | 43 |
| VIII.—Chip-Carving .. .. .. .. .. .. .. .. | | 66 |
| IX.—Ornament and Its Application .. .. .. | | 74 |
| Index .. .. .. .. .. .. .. .. .. .. | | 81 |

# LIST OF PLATES.

| Designs for Carving .. .. .. .. .. .. | *Frontispiece* |
| „ „ Carved Bureau .. .. .. | *facing page* 34 |
| „ „ Chip-Carving .. | *facing pages* 10, 53, 66, 72 |
| „ „ Gothic Carving .. .. .. | *facing page* 43 |
| Examples of 17th and 18th Century Carving | „ 78 |

# WOOD-CARVING FOR AMATEURS.

## CHAPTER I.

### PRELIMINARY.

CARVING in wood is an art in which various advantages are combined, for not only is this art beautiful and excellent in itself, but it may further be regarded in the light of a stepping-stone to greater things. In proof of this we need only glance at the history of some of the most famous painters and sculptors, many of whom, we read, rose to greatness from the practice of the comparatively humble art of wood-carving.

Wood-carving is especially suited to those whose necessary occupations and employments allow them very little leisure to devote to amusements and accomplishments, and whose means do not permit them to spend much money in the one or the other. It is an employment which can be taken up at any time, and can be as easily relinquished; for the carver's fingers, when once facility has been learnt, do not easily lose their cunning from disuse. Although considerable practice, combined with natural aptitude, is necessary to enable anyone to become a

B

really skilful carver, the time spent in cultivating this talent will be by no means wasted, even should nothing beyond the merest mediocrity be attained.

A very slight amount of practice will enable any ordinarily skilful person to do simple carving, which, for the encouragement of beginners, it may be said, is often as pleasing as more pretentious efforts, especially when these are not accompanied by great manual dexterity.

On the score of small cost much might be urged in favour of wood-carving as a recreative art, but beyond calling attention to the fact that a large outlay is not necessary at the commencement, little need be said here. A few shillings will procure all the tools that are really requisite for a beginning, and as the carver will, if he be wise, only get others as he requires them, the additional expenditure is hardly felt.

When discussing the necessary " plant," which includes the tools, materials, and everything which is required in setting up the workshop, various little makeshifts and expedients by which much may be contrived, without any serious outlay, will be suggested.

Wood-carving, which at first sight may seem to resemble in some degree the more mechanical employments of carpentry, nevertheless differs from them in this important particular, that, unlike purely manual pursuits, which can be mastered by anyone possessing a fair amount of intelligence and mechanical skill, it demands, in addition to these qualities, a certain " feeling," or, in other words, talent ; this "feeling," or whatever we may choose to call it, it is obviously impossible to teach ; the germ must at least to some degree be innate in the worker; much, however, may be done in the way of fostering and encouraging it.

Although a knowledge of carpentry will be an aid to the wood-carver, it is not essential. The skill in this line need be but rudimentary, though the greater the acquaintance with it, so much the easier will it be to become an adept in carving work of all kinds.

But it must be understood that a person may be highly skilled in carpentry without having a particle of the taste or talent requisite for artistic carving. However great the natural talent may be, it is three-parts wasted if it be fettered by clumsy fingers, and therefore those who suffer from this defect should make every effort to overcome and correct it. It is also well to acquire a knowledge of the different woods employed, their nature and various qualities, and the purposes to which they are best adapted. Also it would be advisable to learn the names and purposes of the common tools in use amongst carpenters, together with the ordinary technical terms, such as dovetailing, morticing, rabbeting, and such like. By these means the carver will be enabled to give clear and intelligible directions in regard to the materials, etc., which will be required in the course of the work.

While on this subject it may be as well to say here once for all that it is not the intention in the following pages to explain the names and uses of tools which do not specially pertain to the carver's art. Those which are used by other workers in wood may be and undoubtedly are useful to the carver, especially if, as many amateurs do, he wishes to "make up" his own work. If he cannot do so there is rarely any difficulty in getting what is required done by a cabinet-maker, who is to be preferred to a joiner or carpenter, as he is more accustomed to small work. As many ladies now take up carving as an amusement, this course will at any rate commend itself to them.

Although it is impossible to acquire skill, or what has been previously referred to as "feeling," from this or any other treatise on carving, the beginner will be helped over the initial difficulties, or perhaps it should rather be said started on the right way. If the directions are carefully attended to and put in practice there is little doubt that a fair measure of success will be attained. Great skill and power to execute important work cannot be derived from books, or, indeed, from tuition of any kind. They must depend almost entirely on the student's ability and application.

For any work, of course, the first requisites are the tools. These are described in the following chapter.

# CHAPTER II.

## TOOLS.

IT is not at all uncommon for those who have not devoted any attention to practical carving to imagine that the work is done with "some kind of a knife." Let the beginner at once dismiss this notion from his mind, for, with the exception of a special one for chip-carving, to which a chapter is devoted, a knife is not used.

The ordinary cutting tools are chisels and gouges of many shapes and sizes. A complete set of them is out of the question, and is not in the least necessary.

The various carving tools most needful, though few in number, must be selected with great care and judgment, the quality far outweighing the quantity; indeed, a few, let us say twelve or eighteen, really good tools, well cared for, and with which you are thoroughly acquainted, will produce as good work as would a whole chestful.

They are to be bought in "sets," but as these are specially prepared for amateurs they cannot be indiscriminately recommended. Some of them are good, but many are such as no experienced carver could use with satisfactory results. These words of caution are deemed necessary, as it is by no means uncommon for the amateur sets to be much more pleasing in appearance than the more workmanlike tools. These, in comparison, are often rough looking, but the quality is generally better, and

FIG. 1.

the original cost little if any greater. Good carving tools are to be had from any respectable tool dealer if a fair price is paid for them, and as a guide to price, tool dealers' catalogues may be consulted with advantage.

Two dozen tools are as many as are required on first setting up; though a dozen would be a far better number to begin with, as

FIG. 2.

much work can be done with them, and others can be added as required.

It is difficult to say with certainty what the selection should be. but as the most useful tools for ordinary work are flat gouges, four of them, $\frac{1}{8}$, $\frac{1}{4}$, $\frac{3}{8}$, and $\frac{1}{2}$in. sizes, will be a fair proportion.

FIG. 3.

These tools are almost flat, like chisels, but instead of being quite so, have a slight curve, as shown in Fig. 1. Between the flat gouge and that with the "quickest" curve, as in Fig. 2, there are several with varying degrees of sweep, and two of a medium quickness, as in Figs. 3 and 4, may be added in, say, ⅜in. size, as well as one of the "quickest."

FIG. 4.

These latter, when of the smallest size, are known as veiners, from their frequent use in carving the veins or small grooves in leaves. Till some measure of facility has been gained with larger tools, their employment will be found difficult.

Chisels are of two kinds, those with the ends ground straight across, as in Fig. 5, and those with ends as in Fig. 6. These latter

FIG. 5.

are known as skew or corner chisels, and next to the flat gouges are perhaps the most useful tools of the carver. One of each kind of chisel in the smallest ($\frac{1}{16}$in.) and ½in. sizes will be useful, but in these, as indeed in other tools, the selection must chiefly depend on the style of carving the worker prefers.

FIG. 6.

A parting, or, as it is commonly called, a V tool, is another useful one, and is almost indispensable, but at first it is difficult to use properly. From the illustration, Fig. 7, the reason for its familiar designation will be recognised.     The $\frac{1}{4}$in. size will be most useful to the beginner.

All the tools that will be required at first are what are known as "straight."     All varieties are, however, made in both "bent"

FIG. 7.

and "curved," as shown in Figs. 8 and 9.   Their object is to allow of their edges cutting in places which could not be reached with the straight tools.   The curved variety (Fig. 9) is of comparatively little use, as the amateur will find that almost everything he is likely to attempt can be done with straight or bent tools.

FIG. 8.

Fig. 10 shows a tool which for many purposes is extremely useful. It is known as the "bent back" gouge, and like all other gouges is made in a great variety of sweeps and sizes.

If any bent tool is got with the first lot of tools, it should be a bent chisel of the smallest size, as it will sometimes be useful in

FIG. 9.

cutting away the ground in places which could not well be reached by the other tools.

In choosing these tools, do not be too easily satisfied, or inclined to think that the first that is seen will suit, but rather take time and examine each separately until those of the right sort are found ; for, as in other matters, there are tools and tools. Choose, then, those that are long and slender, and of which the points when pressed on the table feel somewhat springy ; they should also

FIG. 10.

be slightly, almost imperceptibly, bent or curved up towards the end ; this curve must not be exaggerated, or it will weaken the tool.

Sets of tools for amateurs are generally sold handled, but for ordinary carvers' tools the handles are supplied separately. They  can be fitted on by the tool dealer ; if, however, the carver prefer to do this, great care must be taken to set them in very straight, as otherwise the tool will not work truly. The handle itself should be small but long, about one-half of the whole length ; this is especially necessary in those tools with which a mallet is used, in order to have plenty of room for the hand to grasp it without fear of being hit. The length of handle for the smaller tools, which are chiefly used without the mallet, must be regulated by the size of the hand, the forefinger of which should rest on or a little below the hilt, while the butt end rests in, and is pushed forward by, the hollow of the palm. The form of ready-made handles is generally round, but an octagonal or hexagon shape, as in Fig. 11, with the thickest part in the middle, rather than at the end, is a

FIG. 11.     very useful variety, as it thus affords a firmer grasp for the fingers. Handles should be made of some hard wood, such as ebony, rosewood, or box, or indeed any wood capable of being made very smooth and highly polished :

if otherwise the palm of the hand would be liable to be galled
by the constant friction and pressure. This is a point of great
importance, and should always be borne in mind, for the very
best carver could hardly fail to turn out bad work when wincing
under a blistered hand, and nothing is so certain to cause this
as an ill-made or rough handle. For this reason it is well to
avoid using a tool the handle of which has been beaten and
frayed with blows from the mallet, without repolishing it with
a file or glass-paper.

If, instead of the modest number of tools we have suggested, a
greater quantity is purchased, it will be found very convenient to
have the handles of various woods and colours, so that each may

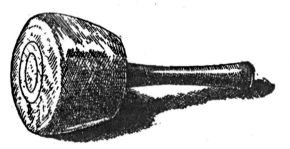

Fig. 12.

be known at a glance; thus, for instance, the smaller gouges
might be of rosewood; the largest, cherry wood; the chisel, ebony,
and others of boxwood; also it is a convenience to have a number,
or any special mark, branded on the handle to denote the size;
by this means no time is wasted in searching for any particular
implement, which would certainly be the case were they all
alike, without any means of distinguishing them. All these little
matters, trivial and hardly worth noticing though they may seem,
are, nevertheless, as long experience has taught, of very material
assistance.

In any but the lightest work a mallet of some kind is necessary,

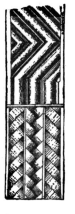

GOTHIC AND RENAISSANCE BORDERS.

DESIGNS FOR CHIP CARVING.

for no tool should be knocked with a hammer. The carver's mallet has a round head, as shown in Fig. 12, but an ordinary one does very well.

Though not an indispensable tool, a router will be found useful

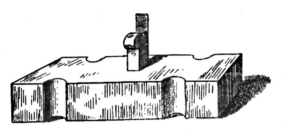

FIG. 13.

in ensuring a level, uniform ground. One variety is shown in Fig. 13, but whatever the details of shape and finish, the principles are alike. All that is essential is a piece of wood, flat underneath, with a hole, through which a narrow steel blade is passed and wedged tightly in any desired position. A very serviceable router can be made with an ordinary screw nail, screwed in the usual way through the wood, filed flat and sharpened to resemble a chisel at the lower end. It can be pushed further through or drawn back as required by a few turns with a screw-driver.

Many tools, but especially the router, are used in levelling

FIG. 14.

the ground on which the carving is in relief, though instead of a perfectly smooth surface, a roughened one is generally preferred. This is got by hammering a punch over the ground, the end of the punch either being filed to a series of points, or having a

fancy pattern at the end.   Though some of these are ornamental,
it may be doubted whether the appearance got by using points
can be improved on for general effect.   Such a punch is shown
in Fig. 14.   A thick French nail makes a very effective one when
the point is filed off and notches are filed across the end.   The
single point of the nail does very well, but of course takes more
time to cover the ground

Bent files, or rifflers, are occasionally useful, but the novice
certainly will have no use for them, and should not get any till
he can feel that they will be of advantage.

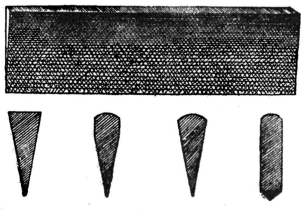

FIG. 15.

An ordinary oilstone, such as is used by joiners, etc., is desirable, and smaller pieces are necessary for sharpening gouges.
These pieces are known as slips, and are sold for the purpose.
They should have the edges curved so as to fit *inside* the gouges,
as shown in Fig. 15.   It is by no means difficult, though somewhat
tedious, to prepare one's own, by splitting up an old oilstone and
rubbing the edges to suitable curves.   Even pieces of slate make
very useful slips.   By having the edges rounded differently, each

slip may be made useful for gouges of widely differing sweeps. About three inches long and one inch wide is a suitable size for a slip. The flat sides may, if necessary, be used instead of the ordinary oilstone. To keep the tools in order a strop is necessary, but this will be found described in the chapter devoted to sharpening tools.

# CHAPTER III.

## WOOD.

AFTER tools, the materials on which to use them stand next in importance. In the choice of these the worker must be guided by the nature and style of carvings he chiefly affects; speaking generally, oak is the best wood for large subjects, and ebony or boxwood for small minute work; but walnut, lime, chestnut (both horse and Spanish), mahogany, and plane are all suited to the purpose; while sandal wood, apple, pear, holly, cypress, fig, and lemon tree, being hard and fine grained, may all be used with good effect, according to the style and size of the carving and other circumstances. Foreign oak is much to be preferred to home-grown wood, which is of a hard and tough nature, and liable to knots, which are a great impediment to the carver, and from which most foreign oak is comparatively free. These oaks may be known by the close and smooth grain and somewhat grey tinge, the English wood being coarser grained and of yellower colour. Oak is especially suited to decorative work in a library or large hall, for ecclesiastical purposes, and for imitation antique carving.

Spanish chestnut and mahogany may be classed next after oak for carvings which though large require a great amount of finish. Of mahogany, there are two very distinct kinds; one of them being comparatively soft—it is known as Bay wood or Honduras mahogany—the other kind is harder and darker, and known as Spanish; many of the works of Grinling Gibbons are carved in this wood, though others are in the softer and less durable lime wood.

American or black walnut is a wood which has come into favour in recent years. It is of moderate hardness, and cuts cleanly. Other walnut wood is not so suitable, though occasionally used.

Sycamore, lime, holly, and woods of a like nature, being white or cream coloured, are only suited to that especial style of carving the beauty of which depends on great purity of colouring; such, for instance, as a minute basso relievo after a picture, models of figures in imitation of ivory, groups of birds, or delicate foliage, such as we sometimes see exhibited in proof of the artist's skill; but all these woods, unless protected by glass, soon lose their extreme whiteness, and with it their chief beauty; therefore they are little used, excepting for the trifling purposes we have just mentioned. The woods of the apple and pear trees are, from the hard texture and fine grain, exceedingly pleasant to work, but their value as productive trees renders them rare, and the occasional deep-coloured veinings sometimes interfere with the design. Box wood is equally hard and fine grained, and is far superior in uniformity of colour, which is a rich yellow. The great bar to the free use of all these hard woods, apart from any difficulty in carving them, is the difficulty of procuring them in pieces of any size, for they are mostly of small growth, rarely attaining to more than 10in. or 12in. in diameter.

Ebony or black wood is very suitable for small carvings of every description, whether for use or ornament, the deep black colour and the hardness and fine texture of grain giving it when polished the appearance of black marble. This wood is also somewhat difficult to procure in large blocks, for it rarely arrives here in logs of any size that are not more or less riven and spoilt by cracks and flaws—"shakes," as they are termed in timber merchants' parlance. There are two kinds of ebony, the green and the black ; but for carving purposes there is little or nothing to choose between them ; though the black is capable of taking a finer polish, its only drawback being an occasional white or red streak. These are rare, and can be easily obliterated by applying a little ink to the spot after the carving is finished.

Sandal wood, from the texture, beautiful colour (a rich yellow brown), and the delicious scent which is familiar to everybody, is especially suited for small carvings. The superabundance of oil, which emits so delightful a fragrance, causes it also to take a beautiful polish merely by rubbing it slightly with the hand. The best sandal wood is brought from India and Ceylon. It also, like ebony, is difficult to procure in sound pieces. It is sold, as are the most valuable woods, by weight. Small pieces are cheaper than large ones in proportion, unless they are prepared and squared to any given size, and then they are far more expensive, as in the course of preparation two or three logs may perhaps be cut up and spoilt before one can be found without flaw, and of course this waste is taken into account and charged for by the wood merchant. Ebony and box wood are sold in the same manner. Each little piece is valued for the smell, even the chips and saw-dust being treasured by some people to burn on the hearth to scent the room.

Ordinary woods—oak, walnut, mahogany, lime, and others—are generally sold by measurement, at so much per foot, varying according to quality and other circumstances, and can be bought in quantities from a timber merchant, or, if only a small piece be wanted, from a carpenter or a cabinet-maker. The hard woods, if the carver live in the country, are more difficult to procure. Occasionally, a turner with a good stock may be found, and he may be willing to sell some ; but this is often an expensive way, therefore it would be wiser, in London or in any large town, to go to timber merchants making veneerings and hardwood a speciality and choose a good stock. If, however, the order is given by writing, describe roughly the dimensions required, as, for instance, 12lb. of sandal wood, 1½ft. long by 4in. or 5in. square, and a log will be sent, out of which such a piece could be cut, weighing perhaps 16lb. or 18lb. This may seem somewhat wasteful at first sight, but in the end will be found to be real economy, for frequently, without the slightest intention of deceiving you, a piece may arrive with half a dozen flaws in it, although when first cut and sent from the warehouse it was to all appearance sound and good; it is well, therefore, to allow a large margin for misfortunes such as this, especially as an ingenious workman suffers nothing to be wasted, but finds some use for every little piece.

It is needless to say that the longer all kinds of wood are kept before being used, so much the better seasoned they will be. We would, therefore, advise all who can conveniently do so, to lay in a stock of those woods which they are in the habit of using. It must, however, be stored up with care, excessive heat and all damp being avoided. If possible, saw out the piece required a short time before the actual carving is commenced, as then any little defect which on first being cut would be imperceptible will be detected. This is a very wise precaution, as nothing is more disheartening and provoking than to be obliged to cast aside work commenced, and on which, perhaps, time and labour have been expended, on account of the material turning out worthless.

It will generally be found that wood got from a dealer of repute is seasoned, but this is not always the same as being dry, hence the necessity of the foregoing caution.

Pine is generally regarded as being too common for carving purposes, but there is no reason why it should be altogether neglected. It is cheap and soft, so that for the beginner it is perhaps the best wood that can be got. If care be taken in selection, it can be got free from knots in sufficiently large pieces. Red or yellow pine should be used, not spruce, which is very knotty and unpleasant to work.

American white wood is another good and cheap wood which has come into considerable use during the last few years. It cuts cleanly, and is remarkably free from knots or flaws of any kind. When suitably stained it is very like American walnut in appearance.

# CHAPTER IV.

## BENCH, AND METHODS OF HOLDING WORK.

WOOD and tools having been dealt with, the remaining appliances necessary for the carver may now be considered. If a room is reserved as a workshop, the light should be good and the bench or table placed near the window, which should face the carver.

A carpenter's bench in miniature is the most suitable form of table for ordinary carving purposes. The size will, of course, vary according to circumstances, and also as regards the style of carving; the minimum size of the bench should not, however, be less than 1½ft. wide, by 4ft. 6in. long; 5ft. 6in., or even 6ft., would be a more convenient length, always provided that there is plenty of elbow room; if otherwise, it will be wiser to have a small table, rather than be cramped in the surrounding space. It should be thoroughly well and strongly made, and capable of bearing rough usage. To ensure this, it must be screwed and pegged as though for a regular workman's bench, and the legs had better be strengthened by a rail from the one to the other, near the floor. These precautions are the more necessary with a small table, which should also be made heavier in proportion, to ensure firmness. The top should be of a good thickness, say 2in.

Should an ordinary table, such as is used in a scullery or pantry, be used, it must be clamped down to the floor, or, if more convenient, to the wall, but better still to both, as the steadier it can be made the better ; no good work can be done if it be shaking and jogging at each stroke.    The ordinary iron angle brackets answer the purpose of clamps very well.

The table given in Fig. 16 is especially adapted for large carvings, particularly for those in full relief, such as the eagle lectern described further on.    As will be seen in referring to the sketch,

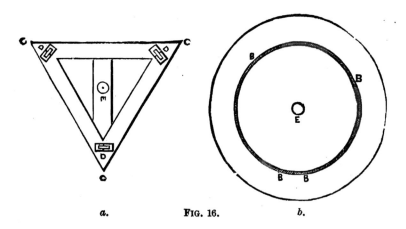

a.                    FIG. 16.                    b.

the top (*b*) is made to turn round, so as to present, at will, every side of the carving to the workman without his being obliged to change his own position.    The great advantage of this is, that he can obtain a strong light on that part on which he is occupied without the loss of time and labour of shifting the subject and fastening it to the bench afresh.    The top of the table in turning carries with it vices, carvings, and all, thus much time is saved. As this kind of table will not easily be found ready made, though to the advanced carver it may occasionally be useful, we give a slight sketch (Fig. 16, *a* and *b*) and description of it, from which any intelligent carpenter would easily make one. The framework of this table, given in Fig. 16, a, is in the form of an equilateral triangle, and must be very firmly and solidly put together ; it should stand upon three stout legs spreading towards the floor, and secured by rungs or cross-pieces about 6in. from the ground ; if a triangle of wood were fixed between the legs about half-way up, it would further strengthen them, and also serve as a convenient shelf for tools, etc.

The top of the table (Fig. 16, b) consists of a solid round of wood 1½in. or 2in. thick, and about 18in. or 2ft. in diameter. This should be strengthened and prevented from warping by two cross-pieces let in flush on the under side and across the grain. The circular groove B is for the three wheels DDD to work in, and should be very evenly and carefully cut, that they may move easily and without obstruction. These three wheels, DDD, as will be seen in Fig. 16, a, are let into the points of the triangle, CCC, and should turn on very strong pins, for they have to sustain the weight of the top, and of the carving, and should be raised above the level of the triangle, in order to enter the groove B. The centre hole E (Fig. 16, b) corresponds with E in the cross-piece of Fig. 16, a, and is for the holdfast (Fig. 18, described a little further on) to pass through ; this is screwed up into the mass of the wood which is being worked, and thus the whole is held firmly together. On requiring to alter the position, the screw beneath is merely loosened, and the top of the table with its burden of wood will turn easily on the wheels DDD. As the greater part of the heavy work, involving the use of the mallet and chisel, is best executed in a standing position, it is convenient to have a table such as this made somewhat higher than an ordinary one, say to stand about 4ft. from the ground, for it is very fatiguing to be obliged to stoop to such work. This table, though by no means a substitute for the common bench, will nevertheless be found an exceedingly useful appendage in the studio of the carver doing large work.

Such an elaborate contrivance is, however, by no means necessary even to the advanced worker, and to the beginner it will be useless. Those who cannot command a work-room and regular bench may be assured that excellent work can be done on an ordinary table provided it is substantial enough to be rigid, or can be fixed in some way, as already indicated. It can hardly be too strongly insisted on that unless the table or bench is sufficiently firm to resist the thrusts against the tool when carving, good work cannot be done. Therefore, those who have not a perfectly firm bench will do well to confine themselves to small carving—such as can be done without moving or shaking the bench or table.

It may be as well to say here that even a table with a good top which one would not wish to injure, such as a dining-table, may be used by the carver.

The next important point to be considered is the method to be adopted for holding the wood while it is being carved, for it must be known that both the carver's hands are engaged with the cutting tool. It is useless to attempt to hold the wood with one hand and to carve with the other.

Although the wood must be rigidly held so that it cannot slip about on the bench top, it is also desirable that it should be easily released and refixed in an altered position, for it is often necessary to do so to get at particular parts.

A good deal depends on the work itself, as to what is the most convenient way of securing it to the bench, and it is impossible to give directions which shall apply equally to each and every case. The carver must use his own discretion, and consider what facilities are available. To guide him, the following suggestions will be sufficient. If an ordinary joiner's bench is used, it will be provided with a bench vice, which may be useful occasionally, but it is so rarely indispensable to the carver that nothing more need be said about it.

For flat work, *i.e.*, panels, etc., by far the most convenient appliance for holding the wood is the "bench holdfast," shown in Fig. 17. It consists of a round bar of iron which passes through a hole made for the purpose in the bench. The arm is hinged on to it, and is raised and depressed by means of a screw working on the top of the bar, fixing the wood firmly to the bench in the required position. To use it, the long portion is passed through the hole in the bench top, the panel is placed under the end of the curved portion, and the screw turned. To prevent the panel being damaged by the iron, a piece of waste wood can be inserted between them.

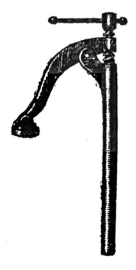

The "woodcarver's-screw," shown in Fig. 18, is another useful appliance of recognised merit for all kinds of carving, and indispens-

FIG. 17.

able to the professional carver.

It is very simple, consisting only of a strong iron screw, which is passed through a hole in the table, into which it should fit somewhat tightly; it is then screwed up into a similar hole bored in the body of the carving, and secured by an iron nut under the table, which, when screwed home, fixes it down to the table as firmly as required; the iron may penetrate into the wood as far as the nature of the carving will permit, the farther the better, as the greater hold it takes so much the more firmness will be insured. Great care must be taken on first boring the hole to guard against injuring the carving, and also to see that the boring is straight.

FIG. 18.

It will often be convenient to have a block of wood with a hole in it for the screw to pass through underneath the bench. This block not only prevents the wood about the hole in the bench being worn away, but saves a good deal of time and trouble otherwise.

The screw, although it may be used for panel carving, is specially useful for work which cannot well be kept in place by the "holdfast."

Apart from the cost, the chief objection—from an amateur's point of view—to both holdfast and screw is the necessity of having a work bench or table used exclusively for such, on

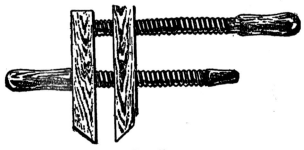

Fig. 19.

account of the hole in the top. This, of course, cannot be allowed on a table, and other means must then be devised for holding the work. That these are not altogether of a makeshift character may be inferred from the fact of professional carvers occasionally using them.

As the protection of the table top is often an object, it may be well to suggest that this can be sufficiently provided for by having what may be called a false top. The size of this piece must depend on that of the wood, which it may be assumed is a panel, being carved. Provided it is larger, nothing more is wanted, so that a piece of boarding 1in. thick and a few inches larger than the panel will do very well.

To hold this board to the table, the ordinary wooden hand-
screws, as in Fig. 19, may be used, and if the carving is sufficiently
far from the edge of the wood, they do well. There is, however,
the objection that the ends of the screws being above the table may
be in the way of the carver. Unless the work is very large, small
iron cramps, of which there are many varieties, are preferable ;
one of them is shown in Fig. 20, and it will be seen that by having
the screw downwards, there is very little projection above, and

even this may be done away with by
cutting a small space in the top of the
carving board. It is seldom that one
cramp will hold this firmly, but as they
are very cheap it is not a serious matter
to have two or three of them. If possible
the board should be placed at a corner
of the table, as it is then so much easier
to secure it.

The work being carved may be
fastened to the board, or simply held
to it in any position that may suit
the carver. In the former case the
position of the board must be altered,
and to do so is not always convenient.
Which is the better plan to pursue the
carver must decide for himself.

If the panel is to be fixed to the
board, it may be managed by means of

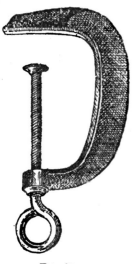

FIG. 20.

screws or glue. The screws are merely driven through from
below the board into the panel. This way does very well
if the screw holes are not a disfigurement, and if the panel is
sufficiently thick for the screw points to hold in it without there
being any risk of the carving tools coming in contact with them.
If screws are inadmissible, glue must be used ; but if the two
surfaces are directly glued together, it will be difficult, if not

impossible, to get them apart again without injury. The way to manage is to glue them together with a piece of paper between. Thus a piece is stuck on the panel and this is then glued to the board. When the work is done, by inserting a knife blade between the two pieces, the paper splits and they come apart. Almost any kind of paper may be used, but none is better than newspaper. It is seldom necessary to glue the entire surface, as a touch here and there at the discretion of the worker is generally sufficient.

It may be as well to remind the novice that it is sometimes useful, even when the holdfast or carver's screw is used, to have a piece of wood fastened on behind the carving; for instance, when

FIG. 21.

the former might damage the carving if laid directly on its face, or when the panel is so thin that the screw could not be used with it.

When it is desired to have the carving movable on the board, the devices that may be used are almost endless in their modifications, and only a few can be suggested.

Three or four screw nails may be driven into the board, close to the edges of the panel, so as to prevent its moving. The heads of the nails clamp the panel down sufficiently. This method seems more cumbersome than it really is, for it is seldom necessary to remove and refix more than one or two of the screws whenever the position of the panel is altered.

A more fanciful method, and one which has some advantages over the foregoing, is to bore a series of holes in the lower board and cut pegs to fit them. With a sufficiency of holes, and a little management, it will be found easy to fix the panel in any desired position with four or five pegs. These should be of sufficient stoutness to resist the thrusts of the carving tools, and must project above the board, so that the panel is against them. A fresh hole can easily be made whenever required.

A more workmanlike plan, and one that is even simpler than the above, is to have one or more wooden catches shaped somewhat as Fig. 21. They can be made as required, and should be of some tough, hard wood. The part cut away for the thickness of the panel should be a trifle less than this, so that on tightening the screw the carving is firmly held.

If loosening and tightening the screw each time the panel has to be moved is objected to, the alternative of having the opening deeper than the thickness of the panel may be adopted. The panel then fits in quite loosely, and can be easily fastened with a wedge or two driven in above the panel. Putting in the wedge below the panel would have the effect of tightening up, but the panel might not lie firmly, *i.e.*, it might give too much under the pressure of the tools. It is in just such instances that the discretion of the carver will come into play. What may be the easiest and best method in certain circumstances may be an awkward and unsatisfactory one in others, and so much is this the case that it may almost be said that an expert carver has no hard-and-fast regulations for fixing work, but varies his methods as occasion requires. All he requires is that the work shall be held sufficiently firm to allow of the tools being used efficiently, and that alterations in position can be made easily and without loss of time. If the novice will remember these general principles he will be saved some perplexity in knowing how to hold any piece of carving he may be engaged on.

# CHAPTER V.

## SHARPENING TOOLS.

DEALERS in tools often profess that they are sent out
"ready for use," which it may be presumed means that
they are ground and sharpened. The novice must be cautioned
against acting on this supposition, for it is rarely indeed
that a tool, even when professedly sharp, is sufficiently so for
the carver's purpose. It cannot be too strongly insisted on that
good work cannot possibly be done with tools which are not
thoroughly and properly sharpened. Inattention to these points
is often the cause of partial failure, and that there may be no
excuse for our readers a special chapter is devoted to the subject.

Before proceeding it will be well for the novice to understand
that there are three processes in connection with putting a cutting
edge to the tools, viz., grinding on a grindstone, sharpening on
an oilstone, and stropping on a piece of leather.

By the first process, which is merely grinding away superfluous
metal, a tolerably sharp but by no means a fine cutting edge is
got. In similar treatises to this the novice is directed how to do
the grinding himself, and there is no doubt that he may manage
to do it successfully. As, however, the work of grinding is not
altogether easy for a beginner and tools may easily be spoiled, it

will be far better to get the tools ready ground from the dealer. The charge for grinding, if any is made, is very trifling, and it must be remembered that re-grinding is seldom necessary—unless the edge gets accidentally broken.

In case the novice has unground tools supplied him, and must rely on himself or the friendly aid of a carpenter to do the grinding, the difference between the edges of an ordinary cutting tool, such as a chisel, and of carver's tools must be noted.

What might be a very good edge for ordinary joinery would not suit the carver. Tools for carving must taper much more gradually, so that they have a more knife-like edge than a joiner's or cabinet-maker's tools. Figs. 22 and 23 represent approximately the two kinds of edges, that required on carving tools being the thinner of the two. If the tools are ground by anyone un-accustomed to the wants of the carver, this difference must be

FIG. 22.        FIG. 23.

insisted on, for, however keen the actual cutting edge may be, satisfactory work cannot be done unless the tools have a long tapered bevel. It is, therefore, at least as important to see that the grinding or initial sharpening is as correctly done as the sub-sequent sharpening on the oilstone. Though this as well as the former requires skill, there is less risk of spoiling a tool by a novice, and if he cannot get a carver to do what is necessary, he need not hesitate to do the sharpening himself. Indeed, the sooner he learns to do so the better, as tools are constantly requiring to be sharpened, and the practice of getting an expert to do this whenever needed is not always convenient. Even if it is, it is far better that the carver should be able to keep the tools in order for himself. If the tools are new, even if they are said to be "sharp," it is often a tedious job to get really satisfactory edges. A good deal of patience may be necessary, but any trouble is justified by the result. When once the tools are right, it is a comparatively easy matter to keep them so. To prevent misunderstanding, it is well that the beginner should know that the edge should be as "sharp as a razor." An edge that would do for even a sharp knife would not do for carving. The tool must cut quite cleanly without tearing or bruising the wood. The work should look as if it had been cut, not as if it had been worried or "gnawed by rats."

By the oilstone all roughness left by grinding must be rubbed down, and no sharp angle must be left where the bevel and the straight part of the blade unite.

Tools should be sharpened on both sides, as in Fig. 22, and not only as in Fig. 23. This especially applies to chisels, as in

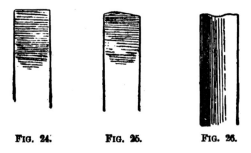

FIG. 24.        FIG. 25.        FIG. 26.

gouges the difference is hardly so decided. When sharpening chisels, care must be taken to keep the bevel straight, as in Fig. 24, and not to let the edge get rounded off, as in Fig. 25.

The sharpening of gouges presents greater difficulty than in the case of flat tools, and the rule may be stated as being that they should be ground on the outside and sharpened on the inside. It is, however, necessary to use the oilstone on the outside at first, to remove the roughness left from grinding, and occasionally afterwards to keep the edge in condition. Great care must be taken with gouges that the edge across from corner to corner is straight, so that if the tool be placed with its edge against a flat surface the whole of the edge will touch. If anything, the corners may be slightly rounded off, but on no account must the edge be irregular, as in Fig. 26. Unless care be taken, such an edge, faulty though sharp, will result from either bad grinding or sharpening.

The best directions the novice can have are that the sharpening should be done evenly, all parts of the edge being sharpened equally. This, although somewhat difficult in practice, may be done by beginning at one end of the stone, against which a corner of the gouge rests, and gradually turning the tool as it is drawn along the stone to the other end, the tool being all the time at right angles to the stone.

This applies to the outside of the gouge. The sharpening proper must be done on the inside, and for this the small slips already referred to must be used. Many amateurs find a difficulty in using these, as the pieces of stone are short, and being held in one hand while the tool is held in the other, unless manipulated properly cuts are apt to occur. To avoid mishaps of this kind, various devices have been suggested. None of them, however, is so satisfactory as the ordinary way, about which there need be no risk if the worker will proceed as follows. Hold the tool in the left hand, with the thumb and forefinger against each corner of the blade. In the right hand hold the stone slip. Keep the left hand steady, and move the right. In other words, rub the stone against the tool, and not *vice versâ*. There is then no danger of the carver cutting himself by the stone slipping off the tool. This, with slight modifications, is the method adopted by all practical carvers, and is far better than any amateurish plan of fixing the slip and rubbing the tool against it.

The sharpening of the V tool is at the best a matter of considerable difficulty, but it is in degree only, as it is treated similarly to gouges, *i.e.*, it is sharpened from the inside.

Care must be taken to have both sides of the V sharpened equally, and to have the apex pointed

In the case of ordinary cutting tools the stone produces a sufficiently keen edge, but not on carving tools. They must be finished off by stropping much in the same way that a razor is stropped. A razor strop, if of the flexible or strap kind, as generally used by barbers, does admirably for carving tools. One which is rigid does not do so well, for the insides of the gouges cannot be reached. Much has been written at various times about preparing strops for amateurs, but they cannot do better than adopt the above suggestion.

Still, any piece of buff leather may be used. It should be prepared by rubbing in a little preparation composed of grease and some very fine powder, such as emery *flour*, putty powder, the finest pumice powder, or even dust. This latter, from its fineness, is the best when the strop has been matured, but with it alone some time is required to get the strop into condition. Emery powder, even when in its finest form of flour, cuts away the tool rather too much if freely used, and as a happy medium between the two extremes, there is nothing superior to jewellers' rouge. Whether this or anything else is used, it is just rubbed into the leather with a little grease of any kind. At most tool shops a "razor paste" is sold in small, collapsible tubes, and does well for the carver.

The strop must never be absent when the carver is at work, for it is in constant requisition, and it is a bad plan to neglect its use. The older it gets the more highly it is esteemed generally, and if the tools are properly used, an occasional rub with the strop will keep their edges in such condition that the oilstone will seldom be required.

Some carvers are in the habit of letting the tools all get dull and then having a general sharpening up; it is necessary to say that this is not a good one, and the carver should make a practice of keeping his tools constantly in best possible condition.

Before concluding this chapter it may be well to give the novice a reliable test by which it may be ascertained whether the edges of the tools are sufficiently sharp. It is very simple, and consists merely in cutting *across* the grain of a piece of soft wood, pine being generally used for the purpose. If the tools cut the wood cleanly, leaving a smooth surface, they are all right. If, however, there is any appearance of roughness from the grain of the wood having been torn through rather than cut, the edges of the tools are not sharp enough, and the carver should not be satisfied with them till they will stand the above test. In conclusion, it may be noted that an edge may be sharp enough to cut a hard wood easily and yet not cut a soft one cleanly. Hence the recommendation to test tools on pine. If they cut it properly they may be used on any kind of wood.

# CHAPTER VI.

## PANEL CARVING.

WHEN the tools are ready the carver will naturally want to begin work with them, but before the actual carving can be commenced the design must be drawn or otherwise marked on the wood. Ability to draw is necessary, as it is almost impossible to conceive of anything like proficiency in carving being attained by a carver who cannot manage to draw the outlines of a design on the wood.

Those who cannot do so may purchase sheets of designs and paste them on the wood. This plan, however, is objectionable in many ways, and it is better to transfer the outlines by means of a hard point and carbon or transfer paper.

About the designs themselves it is only necessary to say that most of those which are published are far too intricate for the beginner to attempt to carve. For him the simpler the design the better, and he must be cautioned not to try anything difficult at first. Too often the novice if left to himself commences a piece of work which would tax the skill of a clever carver, and naturally failing to execute it properly becomes discouraged. The simplest designs if carefully carved are more pleasing than an elaborate design badly executed. In a subsequent chapter (IX.) the beginner will find some further useful hints on this subject.

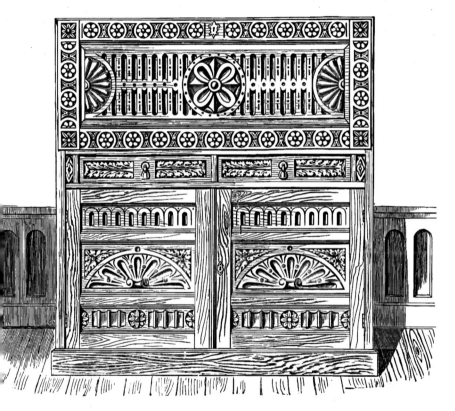

CARVED BUREAU.

Perhaps it may be as well here to remind the beginner that though ability to carve anything in close imitation of nature may indicate a high degree of mechanical skill, no great artistic talent is shown by doing so. It is out of the question to dilate at any length on this point, but the beginner must be dissuaded from, rather than encouraged in copying anything, such as a leaf, a flower, etc., in wood-carving. A more or less conventional treatment is necessary.

Whatever the subject chosen, the actual work, subject to slight modifications, is the same, and for the purposes of exemplification, Fig. 27, which is reproduced from one of Vere Foster's drawing copies, may be taken. Many similar subjects may be got from Vere Foster's (published by Blackie and Son) or any other good series of drawing copies. They will afford excellent outlines for working from, and for the beginner at any rate are far superior to the designs specially published for amateur wood-carvers.

For the wood, none can be better than pine, sound and free from knots. A piece ⅜in. thick will be sufficient. Although not absolutely essential that the surface should be smooth, it is better to have it planed over. The design can be more clearly seen, but a more important reason is that dust and grit may have settled on the rough surface, and these would have a very prejudicial effect on the tools.

The first thing is to get the outline carefully drawn on the wood, and it may be as well to say here that the smaller the work the greater will be the difficulty in carving it. The design we are taking should not be less than the size of this page, and the wood should be at least 2in. larger each way.

An experienced carver might now cut in tne outlines with a V tool or veiner, but the novice certainly could not hope to use this with any chance of success. He must adopt an easier method. It is to cut down on the line with tools the sweep or curve of which most nearly conform to the design. The tool is held upright in the left hand and knocked into the wood with the mallet, to the depth of say ½in. With a limited stock of tools it will be impossible to keep accurately to the line, but by letting the cuts overlap, as shown in Fig. 28, a very close approach to

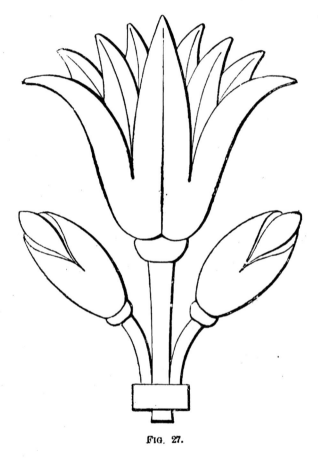

FIG. 27.

accuracy can be made. Small irregularities can be trimmed off afterwards. The next process is to cut away some of the waste wood with a gouge sloped down to the perpendicular cut, going all round the design. While doing this the work must be firmly

held by one or other of the means already described. The panel
will then look something like Fig. 29, where the notches made by

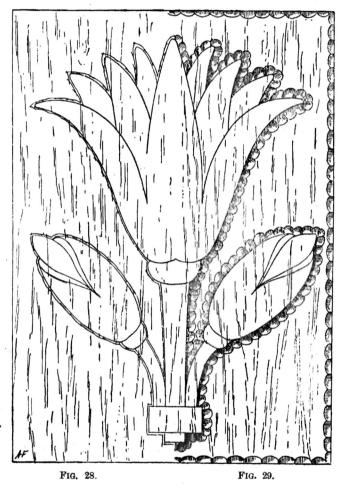

FIG. 28.                    FIG. 29.

the gouge are clearly shown. If the cuts made are not deep enough,
the outline must be gone over again, hammering down with the
mallet as before, and repeating the notching.

The next proceeding is to cut away the waste wood. This is generally best done with a flat gouge, but any that are most convenient may be used. Care should be taken to keep all parts as nearly uniform in depth as possible. This can be managed very well by the router. Its blade is set projecting from its stock to the required depth of the ground. By then working it in all directions the ground is scraped level and to an equal depth, the stock working on the raised or uncut portion of the design. This now looks very much as if it had been fret-cut and stuck on a flat piece of wood. If preferred, the ground may be trimmed quite smooth with a flat gouge or chisel, but it is seldom necessary to do so, as any roughness or tool marks will be hidden by the subsequent punching.

The really difficult part of carving and that on which the artistic merit of the work depends now begins. The raised flat portion must be " carved " or moulded, and care must be taken in doing this not to tear the wood—as far as possible the cutting should be with the grain. At first the carving should be done to get the general contour without any attempt at finishing, gradually trimming up the work with light and delicate cuts. If, as is very likely, the edges of the design have got damaged, or there seems a want of relief, the work may often be much improved by undercutting a little, so that the edges slightly overhang. This with skill may be done with the skew-chisel, of which the obtuse angle should be presented to the wood ; but an easier way will be to cut downwards very much as when stamping in the outline. This undercutting will have the effect of throwing the carving up, but must be done judiciously.

The final process is to punch the ground. This is managed with the punch, held in the left hand, and knocked with the hammer in the other.

On the Frontispiece will be found some designs for panel carving. Fig. 30 is a slightly conventional treatment of the vine, the leaves and fruit are almost true to nature in themselves, but the growth line and the disposition of the foliage are in conformity with the space to be occupied. The grapes should not be carved to project as much as they would in nature, but should be kept in low relief. If it is not beyond the skill of the worker, a great improvement will be effected in the appearance if a certain amount of under-cutting is introduced. This can be done at the crossing of the stems and at the edges of the leaves. It may be that the leaves in this case would tax the skill of the amateur somewhat, and if desirable the more conventional treatment of the leaf shown in Fig. 32 may be substituted. If this is done the growth line and fruit should also be conventionalised to a like degree.

Fig. 31 is a design introducing a grotesque with foliated swags and drops. It would be suitable for a panel of an overdoor or of a fireplace. The drops may be extended to suit any special position, such as the surround to a mirror. The carving as drawn is in high relief ; but if desirable it may be carried out in low.

In Fig. 32 the design is for a carved frieze suitable for ecclesiastical work. The flow of the growth line is horizontal in this case, and is contained between two lines of moulding. The more the background is cut away the better will be the effect.

A soft-grained wood will be found most suitable for all of the above. In all of these examples will be seen the principle of so arranging and disposing the object or objects selected, that the space to be treated becomes, not a background for a botanical study, but a definite design. The subject is referred to later in Chapter IX., and too much attention cannot be paid to it.

Fig. 33 is an example of a very effective and simple method of decorative carving. The design, which is an easy geometric one, is formed by cutting away the spaces between to a depth of about ¼in. The background thus formed may be treated in a variety of ways in order to give prominence to the actual lines of the design, which is left plain. Although the illustration is for a panel suitable for a newel-post or other similar position, the ornament may be continuous and used on a frieze or a dado. Many examples of the use of this type of design will be found in furniture of the

Fig. 33.

Chippendale period and a careful study of these will provide a fund for the worker to draw upon.

It is usual to give the novice much advice as to the way the tools should be held, but really very little that is likely to help him can be told. The most convenient way in which to do so can only be learnt by practice, for the movements are constantly varying. As a rule very little can be done with one hand only. Both hands must hold the tool, one, the right, supplying the force, the other being mainly used to guide and restrain. To

FIG. 34.

explain more in detail, the tool is held by the right hand over the handle, and the left hand rests more or less on the work, with the fingers round the blade of the tool, which is thus controlled. Fig. 34 shows the position, which it will be seen allows the tool to be used with sufficient freedom, and yet easily controlled. There is, however, no necessity to hold it always in this way, for if preferred, and if more convenient, one or three instead of two fingers, or even the whole hand, may grasp the tool. The principle remains the same, and a very moderate amount of practice will

soon convince the beginner that a set of directions how to hold
the tool would hamper rather than aid him. Wood-carving is
distinctly an art, and cannot be learned by rote, beyond a very
elementary stage.

It will probably occur to the beginner to use glass-paper to
finish off his work with. It seems such an easy way to remove
roughness. The use of glass-paper is, however, to be deprecated.
It may be beneficial occasionally, and we are far from saying that
it must never be used, but its employment should be the result of
knowledge and in great moderation. So objectionable is it considered that most writers forbid its use altogether. Certainly for
ordinary work it should not be used, as a piece of carving with
marks of the tools showing is generally preferable to a piece of
work smoothed over with glass-paper. In connection with this one
point must be emphasised, and that is never to use glass-paper on
any work which is afterwards to be touched with the carving
tools. The reason is that the hard dust from the paper being in
the fibres of the wood will quickly blunt and spoil the keenness
of the edges.

DESIGN FOR GOTHIC CARVING.

# CHAPTER VII.

## Various Examples for Carving.

HAVING now a fair idea how to do general carving, examples requiring somewhat different treatment and more experience may be given, merely remarking that the object of the accompanying designs is not so much to give detailed copies as to guide the novice.

Fig. 35 represents a handle for a paper-knife. Should the carver spoil it, neither the time nor the outlay is sufficiently serious to make the loss of any moment. The size of the wood required is 13in. long, 1¾in. wide, and ¾in. thick. The effect is extremely good carved either in ebony, sandal wood, or box.

Having sawn the wood to the required size, examine it carefully to make quite sure that it is sound ; then, being satisfied on that point, proceed to mark the design on it as already explained. If ebony or any dark wood be used, the outline is not easily perceived, and it will therefore be necessary to draw the design on thinnish paper, and gum or paste this upon the wood itself; taking care that every part of the paper adheres thoroughly. When the paper and wood are both quite dry, fix the wood tightly into the vice, and begin to work on the blade of the knife with a spokeshave. It must be scraped down gradually and circumspectly, first on one side and then on the other, taking great care not to shave it away too much in one place; the edge of the blade should run in a perfectly straight line with the handle, or it will not balance. To ensure this it is well to mark three lines down the edge of the blade before any wood is shaved off; one line should be exactly in the middle to represent the sharp cutting edge when finished, and the two others, one on each side, rather less than an eighth of an inch from the centre one; then, either with the saw or the spokeshave, cut away the wood down to these two outer lines, and roughly shape out the form of the blade; then leave it until the time comes for finishing it off, which will be

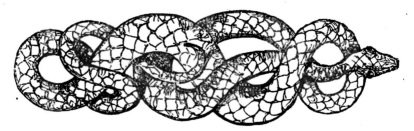

FIG. 35.

when the handle is about three-parts done, when a rasp or coarse file may be used to get it into shape. Files are better than any tools for the purpose, as with them the blade can be gradually reduced without fear of spoiling it by taking off too much. The edge of broken glass will also be found very useful for the same purpose. The blade of a large paper-knife, such as this, ought when finished to be one-third of an inch in thickness in the thickest part, that is, where it joins the handle; from there it should slope gradually and easily down to the point and cutting edges; these latter should be perfectly free from notches in the wood or unevenness of any kind; nor should they be over sharp, or they will soon split and break off.

So to return to the handle, which has been left untouched, saving the design gummed or traced upon it. The first thing required is to cut away carefully all the waste wood in between the coils of the snake on the outside. Make the indentations exactly at right angles with the surface of the design, or you will get into trouble when carving the reverse or underside. Having done this, take the drill, and make one or more holes, according to the space, in each part which requires perforation, though, if preferred, this part of the work may be done with a fret saw. Then, with a knife, or if the wood be fixed in a vice, with a chisel, trim the edges away nearly, but not quite, up to the inked edge of the design. When this has been done roughly, go over it again, marking slightly but distinctly where the different parts of the snake cross each other. When the general idea and shape have been thus given, examine it carefully in detail, and ask before proceeding further, such questions as, "Is this part right?" "Does that coil lie naturally?" "Am I leaving too much here, or cutting away too much there?" and so forth; do not dash and slash at it, but *think* in this manner as the work proceeds, and work gradually and cautiously up to the desired end. A good carver is always thinking in this manner, and never does a stroke without a good reason, for carving and sculpture are not like painting, or even modelling, where a false stroke can be obliterated; for a little splinter once nicked off the snake is gone for good, and the reptile looks wrong and woodeny for the rest of its days. Having fashioned it carefully but roughly in the manner described, take a coarsish file all over it, guarding particularly against cutting away too much, for fear of making it look attenuated, remembering that the size of the body is very considerably reduced by cutting and marking the scales, so that before this process is commenced it should look unnaturally plump and fat; and also bear in mind that in life the coils of the snake in crossing yield equally the one to the other, falling together and flattening each other, as it were, with an undulating appearance, and not crossed as so many sticks. Beginners are very apt to fail in this point. To obtain at once a correct idea, which is very essential for the execution of a life-like carving, we strongly advise the carver to copy from life. This rule applies always when carving from nature, whether animate or inanimate, but is especially necessary to observe in regard to the former. Five minutes' examination would be of more service to the carver than a whole chapter of descriptions and directions. When the form has been cut out with tolerable accuracy, go over it all with a file fine enough to render the surface smooth, but not polished. The scales must be marked

FIG. 36.

with a pencil, or scratched with a fine point, an inch or so of the body at a time if the pencil be used, or the marks will rub out. For cutting them, use either the sharp point of a knife or gouges of the right size. From the size and form of the scales varying in each turn, it is necessary if the gouges are used to be constantly changing from one size to another. It is of importance to recollect that not only does each ½in. of the reptile vary in size, increasing from the head to the middle, and decreasing in like manner towards the tail, but also that the size of the scales increases and decreases in the same proportion. Moreover, that on the inner parts of the curves they are small and short, and on the outside exactly the reverse, that is, large and elongated, stretched out as it were. When the scales have been roughly denoted rectify mistakes and irregularities; and again go over the whole, this time more carefully, and trim and shape the edges, obliterating tool marks, and define each separate scale, so that they all lie equally and lightly the one over the other. This done, the paper-knife may be considered as finished, and only requires polishing. For this purpose very fine glass-paper, which has been already well worn, may be used.

To carve Fig. 36, the same directions as above should be obtained as regards the blade and the snake which is twisted round the branch. This design is somewhat more difficult, but has an admirable effect when well carved. In preparing the wood, allowance must be made for the extra thickness; in fact, the part for the handle must be nearly square, about 1½in. each way would not be too much, as it is always better to allow rather over than under the measurement required. As regards the branch round which the snake is coiled, there will be no difficulty in finding a natural model (a little spray of oak or hedgethorn is the best for the purpose); the design will indicate where the knots and branches shall spring from the main stem, but the natural model will teach the peculiar

FIG. 37.

angle and form they take better than can be given in the drawings. In so minute a piece of carving as this the bark can be very successfully imitated by wriggling the edge of a flattish gouge or chisel held nearly uprightly along the surface of a branch. This conveys the idea of irregularity and roughness.

Fig. 37 is another paper-knife design also very effective, and not a little quaint, which to some people is no inconsiderable recommendation. It should be carved in ebony, as it looks better in that wood than in any other. It takes a very solid piece, from 12in. to 13in. long, and 1¾in. square for the handle. This is rather thicker than absolutely necessary, but it is well to be on the safe side. The principal point to bear in mind is that the bird be balanced well and naturally on its perch, and not appear to cling on to it by its tail. The mere roughing out is very easily done. The same care must be bestowed on the blade, which should, if anything, be somewhat thicker, to correspond with the extra thickness of the handle. The feathers are the only difficult parts; the breast should not be smooth, as it is with some birds, but ruffled and lumpy here and there. Owls are always untidy in this respect. It must be clothed with fluff, which, being of an indefinite substance, is best given by the wriggling motion of the tool, described above. This gives that dishevelled appearance of the feathers peculiar to the owl when disturbed and awoke in daylight and obliged to open its eyes. The latter must be set very deeply in two saucers of fluffy feathers, which set out from the eyes like fans, and should be done in the same manner as the breast feathers, with the addition of a few touches of a knife here and there to give decision. The eyes themselves should be left prominent and round, like beads, and polished brightly. The wings and tail feathers should be carefully drawn and marked out with a very small gouge, and ought to lie over each other lightly at the back; a model might be bought, and thus a faithful copy made from nature—a stuffed one will answer the purpose quite as well as if it were alive. The claws must be slightly exaggerated and highly polished; as also the bill, which must be high and hooked, and sunk deeply into the breast fluff.

Fig. 38 is a rustic frame for a miniature or photograph. The ground between the cord and the edge may be gilt or left smooth, according to taste, but the former is the more effective, and indeed

FIG. 38.

E

the easier, when once the trifling manual difficulty of gilding has been overcome; directions for doing which we shall give further on. Should you decide on gilding it, the ground, after being fairly smoothed with the gouge, might be stamped or pricked.

It is often useful to fret-cut a design and stick it when carved on a plain wood ground, as this method is much easier than carving from the solid, or " grounding out " in the manner already described. The effect is very much the same, though fret-cutting and gluing the carving may almost be regarded as a makeshift, and is therefore sometimes objected to. This method is, however, often resorted to.

The correct way to manage is to glue the fretted work to a temporary ground of pine or any cheap wood, to afford support while it is being carved. It is afterwards removed and permanently glued to the proper ground. To allow of its being removed with the least risk of breakage, to which there is always a liability unless the work is bold and strong, a piece of paper glued on both sides is put between the fretted work and the temporary ground. When the carving is done, it can be removed by inserting a thin knife blade, as the paper easily splits.

While on the subject of fret-sawing it may be well to observe that plain fretwork may often be considerably improved and have additional interest given to it by the surface being appropriately carved.

To return to the actual carving. The best way will be to have four pieces of thoroughly well-seasoned wood carefully dovetailed the one in the other, so as to form a diamond; this requires nicety and exactness to render the joins as invisible as possible, or they will spoil the effect of the work. The grain of the wood should run down each piece, otherwise it will not be strong. No rule can be laid down as to size, as it depends entirely on the carver's own fancy and convenience; but supposing that the frame stands 10in. high, the right proportion for each piece would be 7in. long, about 3in. wide, and a little under 1in. in thickness. The first thing to be done is to cut out the oval very exactly. before pasting on the paper design. You must spokeshave or otherwise reduce the outside edge in a gradual slope from the oval to somewhat less than half an inch in thickness. This done smoothly and evenly, proceed in the same manner as described before, being careful to keep a well-drawn copy always at hand to work from. In sawing out the oval, be very careful that the edge is kept square, and have at least a quarter of an inch to spare of margin all round, in case of accidents ; for it is always easy to cut away too much, but difficult to replace it when once it is gone. The design is a hop-vine, twined in an oval form. This can easily be altered, if desired, to suit any other shape—square, round, or three-cornered if preferred. It is drawn from nature, which has been followed very carefully, especially in regard to the manner in which the long, straight stalks cross the foliage. It is in this that the chief difficulty lies. Do not attempt to cut them clear of the leaves until quite the last, when you put the finishing touches ; then do it very gently and carefully with a very small gouge. It requires no small amount of patience to cut them all clearly and cleanly without an accident, for they will, if jambed or pressed in any way, infallibly split off. To work from the stalk down towards the leaf is the safest plan, and never forget for an instant the direction of the grain.

The sharp notching of the leaves is the next difficulty. These, to insure against accidents, should all be marked out with a file. A knife may be used, after the file has done its work, to sharpen the edges ; for this the slightest touch will suffice, provided the knife be really sharp. This design is not a very easy one, but is very beautiful when well carved. It would be easier if it were enlarged, say to double the size ; it might then be done in oak or chestnut. The same design, with a few additions, might be carved on a still larger scale for a chimney glass, and with a flat gilt margin on the inside would look extremely handsome. Having

thus recommended the reader to heighten the effect of his handi-
work by an occasional admixture of gold, after the manner of
ancient carvings, especially those found in Italy, it will not be out
of place if we assist him with a few hints on the subject, so as
to render him independent of the professional gilder, there being
nothing to prevent his acquiring the knack of gilding quite sufficiently for his purpose.

In advocating this practice we may incur the displeasure of
purists, who object to it as meretricious ; but it must also be
remembered that we have the best authority for the use of gold
in this manner.   We have no scruple in recommending it to the
amateur, to whom, amongst other advantages, it acts as a most
acceptable cloak, by rendering the general effect of crude handi-
work passable and even good.

The materials and tools required for the simple process of gilding are few.   In the first place, procure a book or two of gold leaf.
A gilder's tip, which is formed of long hairs set in cardboard, and
looks like a small tooth comb, will be required, as well as a pad
on which to cut the leaf.   The leaf must be cut with a knife, a
common table knife will do, but it must be very smooth edged,
for the slightest notch will tear the gold ; a rather large camel's-
hair painting brush is necessary to fix the leaf in its place, and
two or three common soft-haired brushes also will be wanted to lay
on the size and paint.   All the materials can be bought at oil and
colour shops.

The part to be gilded should be made as smooth as possible,
before giving it the first coat of white paint, having previously
dusted it with a brush.   When the paint is perfectly dry, rub it
with glass-paper to a smooth surface, then paint it again in the
same manner, letting it dry very thoroughly, and repeat this
process three or four times until nothing of the wood can be seen,
but only an even smooth surface of paint ; then coat it over very
thinly with the gold size, and leave it until it is nearly dry, so
that only a very slight stickiness remains, then take the gold leaf

CONSOLE BRACKET.

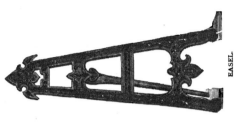

EASEL.

PHOTO FRAME.

FLOWER-POT STAND.

DESIGNS FOR CHIP CARVING.

gently out of the book, and place it on the chamois leather cushion, and cut it into squares or strips according to convenience ; this done, take the comb-like brush and pass it over your cheek or hair. This will cause the leaf to adhere to it until it reaches the surface made sticky by the size. Be very careful to put it into the right position on the first placing, for once there it cannot be removed ; also avoid touching the edge of the knife or the pad with the bare hand, for the gold will adhere to either, and get torn and spoilt. When the gold is in its place, stipple it down on the surface with the painting brush and blow away the loose gold ; a very little practice will soon give the necessary dexterity, patience and a light hand being all that are really needed. While laying on the gold it is absolutely necessary to keep all windows and doors shut, and to prevent people going in and out of the room, as the draught caused by the sudden opening of a door might blow away the leaf, and the leaf once crumpled up becomes useless. When the whole is gilded, dust it with a soft brush to remove and fix stray pieces of gold.

But to return to our present designs. Fig. 39 is a group of ivy leaves covering the end of a book slide. The proportions are somewhat large, suitable for full-sized books. The dimensions of the wood required are 6¼in. by 8in., and 1¼in. thick in the centre, the grain running down the length. Reduce the wood on one side from the original thickness in the centre to half an inch at the edges, so that the leaves when carved may have the appearance of growing and falling over a boss in the middle. The veinings of the leaves must be sharply defined and indented, in order to throw a deep shadow ; but as ivy leaves grow in every hedgerow, the worker can pluck and study them himself. Observe each indentation and peculiarity of shape, and render it as carefully as possible ; it is in minor matters that the talent of a carver is mainly exemplified.

Many other designs suitable for this useful ornament will doubtless occur to the carver ; one perhaps being an animal's head,

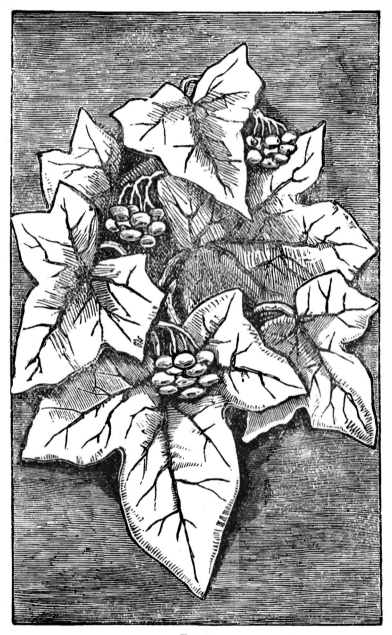

FIG. 39.

another an heraldic crest, and so on. There are few more beautiful subjects for the carver than that of birds, and it is one which can be used in a variety of manners, either purely as an ornament to lay on a slab, or to hang up against the wall, or as a panel for a cabinet or sideboard. For the latter purpose half relief will be sufficient; for the former, three-quarters, or even entire relief is desirable.

It were useless for us to attempt to give any design of this description, for nothing short of a photograph or a most minute engraving could delineate the description and texture of the feathers; but this, however, is of little importance, as the natural bird is about the best model that can be had, and this is within the reach of everyone; but we would remind all those who intend to study from models of this kind that it is preferable to do so in the winter, for not only will it longer retain its original pose, but the worker will not be tempted to hurry over his work for unsavoury reasons. All difficulties of this kind, however, may be avoided, and skill in carving materially improved if a knowledge of modelling in clay be attained. This cannot be too strongly emphasised, as not only does the power to model enable us to retain forms in our memory for future use, which either by nature or circumstances are fleeting—such, for instance, as a specially beautiful group of leaves or flowers, which, even could they be gathered without destroying their pose, would wither before they could be expressed in wood—but with it will develop that sense of feeling which is so desirable. Or, again, to return to the case in point, modelling is invaluable to enable the artist to catch the general outline of a bird, or a group of birds or other animals, while they are fresh, before they become stark and stiff. It may be argued that a slight pencil sketch would answer the purpose as well as a clay model, and with less expenditure of time and trouble, but it is not so, for a few skilful touches in clay will convey an idea such as would be useful to the carver far better than could be done with the pencil, unless it were in very talented hands; moreover, as the rudiments of carving and modelling are the same (which is not the case as regards drawing), it is probable that to express an idea in clay would be easier to the carver than to do so by means of the pencil.

A good quantity of modelling clay can be bought for a mere trifle. It can usually be procured at any pottery works, pipe makers, or at cast shops; but in this latter place it is generally more expensive. It is sold in the form of powder mixed with rough lumps; these must be thoroughly crushed, and the powder worked up with water into a smooth dough, which should be as stiff and dry as is compatible with its being easily handled, for the moister it is, so much the greater will be the risk of its cracking when the water evaporates. The model, when you are not at work on it, should be kept damp with a wet handkerchief or rag thrown over it; if this precaution be neglected, it will dry unevenly and fall to pieces. The same clay can be broken up and used over and over again, by taking care to grind it finely before mixing it afresh. The few tools and instruments required for modelling are very simple and inexpensive, merely little sticks of wood or ivory with different shaped knobs at the end, others, again, being pointed and curved. Half a dozen of the ordinary shapes would do to start with, and with the aid of a knife and some glass-paper, a modeller could easily make as many others as necessity or fancy suggested, the chief point being to make them very smooth, that the clay may not adhere to them.

An excellent substitute for clay, and one which possesses the advantage of being permanently plastic, is a preparation known as " Plastacine." This material may be obtained from any dealer in artists' materials, and although the cost is more than that of ordinary clay, its use will be found a cleaner and more satisfactory method of obtaining the desired result. Plaster of Paris is useful for making a cast from the clay model, if such is needed.

The next design, Fig. 40, is an eagle, for a lectern. The original carving from which this drawing is taken was executed chiefly from nature. It measures 4ft. across the wings, and stands 4ft. 4in. high, irrespective of the ball on which it is placed. This is, however, an unusually large size, it being intended for a cathedral; from 22in. to 30in. across the wings are the usual dimensions. Before commencing this, or any large work of a similar nature, it is advisable to make a small working model of the subject; this model should be made to scale, that is, it should bear a certain proportion to the large work, as, for instance, should it be proposed to make the eagle 24in. across, then let the model be 8in., that is, 4in. to the 1ft. It need not, of course, be highly finished, the minor details of feathering, claws, etc., being of no account, as the sole object is to arrive at a just idea of the general effect, and to satisfy yourself that the pose and proportions are correct, before commencing on the wood itself; of course, should you copy from a model the size of your own carving, these preliminaries will not be necessary; it is only when you are called upon either to greatly increase or reduce its proportions, that this extra work is advisable. A very expert carver might even dispense with it altogether, but it would be extremely rash in a novice to do so, for, as we have elsewhere remarked, carving cannot be altered at will, not at least to any extent, therefore the greater caution used so much the greater will be the chance of success.

To make a rough model, such as described, of the eagle in Fig. 40, it will be necessary, on account of the soft yielding nature of the clay, to form it on a kind of frame, a skeleton, so to speak, which will give it strength to bear its own weight. Fig. 41 represents such a skeleton, which consists of five strips of wood nailed or tied firmly together and fixed into a square of wood so as to form a solid base on which to stand the two side pieces. A A are tied strongly to the cross-piece C in front, while the middle piece, E, passes in front of C in a slanting position, to form the slope from the breast to the extremity of the tail; the head, from being thrown back in the act of looking upwards, balances and supports its own weight. Some carvers prefer to make their models in soft wood, such as deal or willow, and this plan has certainly the advantage, in that it is more durable than either clay or plaster, but it is not so satisfactory on the whole,

Fig. 40.

as in the latter materials the form can be altered and re-altered until it is quite to the artist's mind, which cannot be the case in wood.

Be very careful in superintending the preparation of the wood, and the manner in which it is joined together. This should be entrusted only to a very skilful workman, and one who thoroughly understands his business, for the beauty and success of the work will mainly depend on the exactness and strength with which the parts are put together. Much judgment and care must be expended in the arrangement of the joins, in order that they may interfere as little as possible with the carving itself, as, for instance, the head should be in one piece, that is, with a join on either side, and not in the middle, and so on.

The wood should be cut out of the block and exposed to the air for as long a time as is possible, before it is built up, the longer the better, as the chance of warping, which would be fatal

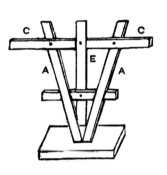

FIG. 41.

to the work, is greatly lessened by many months' exposure. Flaws and knots in the wood itself, though by no means desirable, are comparatively of little importance, as from the boldness and freedom of the design much is left to the artist's fancy, so that any little local flaw can be worked in and concealed amongst the irregularities of the plumage. There is yet one other point which requires attention before the wood is finally clamped together, and this is to place those pieces side by side which agree the best in colour and grain. The shades of the different blocks should blend together so as to give the semblance as far as may be of the eagle being carved out of one entire piece ; carelessness in this respect cannot be atoned by the finest carvings, for all the artist's skill could not save the bird from appearing patchy and woodeny if a stripe of lighter colour than the rest ran down the breast. This is a misfortune which the most ignorant novice can with a little care and painstaking avoid.

In regard to the actual manual part of the subject, it is useless to lay down any rules for the artist's guidance, as it is better in these comparatively minor details that he should work in accord-ance with his own comfort and convenience. As a broad rule, however, it is always well to "rough out" the subject uniformly, and to avoid entering into detail, so as to arrive as soon as may be at a just idea of the general effect, and afterwards to go over it again with a little more exactitude, repeating this process until it stands completed as regards the pose and main features, but devoid, in the case of the subjects in question, of plumage and such like *minutiæ*. These should then in their turn be roughly delineated, and gradually be worked up together into a perfect whole. It is only by rigidly following out this plan that a uniform and natural effect can be obtained by the inexperienced workman ; if, for instance, one wing were highly finished in all its points before the other was begun, the greater part would probably have to be altered, or, as very likely this would be impossible without cutting away two much of the wood, the two wings would look as if they did not belong to the same bird, and the effect of the whole carving would be spoilt. Doubtless, this manner of work-ing up the whole by slow degrees is somewhat a trial of patience, especially if it be a first work of the kind, for it certainly is very tempting to finish up a little bit in order to see the effect. This, though satisfactory for the moment, will spoil the appearance of the finished work, or at any rate is a great risk on account of the danger of cutting away too much of a particular part before it is possible to judge of the whole.

The feet and head of the eagle will require great care, especially the former. Procure, if possible, a real foot as a model. If an eagle's cannot be obtained, that of a smaller bird of prey must do duty. Bestow much pains on observing and imitating the rough-ness of their texture and the manner in which the fluff falls over and round them. The eagle may be designed to stand on a ball of wood, or upon a rock, but be sure that you do not carve or draw a fancy rock out of your own head, for unless you are well practised in such matters it will assuredly be stiff and conventional; but look about and find a real stone, to which, if too large to move, take your modelling clay and copy it faithfully on the spot, and afterwards at home model your eagle upon it. If the worst comes to the worst, and you cannot light on either rock or stone which is suitable, you might find a worse model for your purpose than a piece of coal, which is in everyone's reach. Take care in placing the model on the rock that the claws really clutch it, and that the bird is properly poised and balanced upon it.

We will now pass on to the last and perhaps the most difficult branch of the art—that of carving in basso relievo. For this a knowledge of drawing is almost a necessity, as is also the rudiments of perspective; we say *almost* necessary, for in some rare cases the artist's eye is so intuitively accurate that he can afford to dispense with such knowledge, and may trust solely to an acute feeling of proportion and form to guide him aright; but this is very exceptional, therefore it would be well for those who intend to pursue this branch to practise drawing from casts, if obtainable, and to make the rules of perspective a preliminary study. We would especially counsel ladies to follow this particular line of art, which, while necessitating skill of the highest order, involves the expenditure of less actual strength than those carvings which are in full relief.

The student in this style has an abundance of beautiful and suitable subjects at his command, for not only are casts of most of the best works of this kind procurable, but there is also another field open to him in the many pictures and parts of pictures which are now placed within our reach by means of photography. We would not, however, counsel him to attempt to carve from a flat object, such as a picture, until he has first practised both carving and drawing from a cast, in order to educate the eye in the perspective of figures for this especial purpose. No better models can be found than the casts from the basso relievos of Lucca della Robbia, and others, in the Victoria and Albert Museum. After having worked thus from casts, the next step in advance is to do so from photographs of basso relievo sculpture ; from thence you may, if you wish, pass on to carve from photographs of pictures. Having arrived at this point, your choice of subjects is practically unlimited. Choose, to begin with, a bold and somewhat severe outline, such, for instance, as some of Ary Scheffer's figures ; carved pictures of this kind are, when artistically executed, very beautiful, and the edge of the wood bevelled and finished with a simple ogee, being generally sufficient margin to set off the carving. They present, when finished, the appearance of the picture or figure, being set in saucers or basins of wood, varying in depth according to the taste of the carver, and may be either round or oval, whichever is most suitable to the subject. For small picture carvings of this kind, a flat or slightly bevelled rim of velvet, laid on the wall about 1in. or 2in. in width, is a great improvement, and sets it off wonderfully. This style of wood sculpture was much practised in the 16th century, especially in Spain, where there are many specimens of the kind still preserved ; these also, in many instances, bear marks of the background having been gilded, and even painted in colour. Whether the latter was an improvement is, we think, questionable, but as regards the former there is little doubt that the gilding adds considerably to the effect of the carving, as the reflection of the gold on the convex background marks the outline and throws it into greater relief. Any good single head set thus, as it were, in a round dish or saucer of wood, would be an excellent study, and form also an extremely handsome object in a room, hung picturewise on the wall ; you will find some very beautiful heads suited for this purpose on the doors of the Baptistry at Florence, a full size model of which is in the South Kensington Museum ; excellent photographs have been taken of the original, from which a good carver could easily work.

To find good casts is a somewhat more difficult matter, especially for those who live in the country, for in London, at the Victoria and Albert Museum, you can at any rate see, even if you cannot buy them ; occasionally pretty good models may be bought at

Messrs. Brucciani & Co., 258, Goswell Road, London, E.C. The plaster of Paris images which are offered for sale in the streets would very probably mislead rather than guide and improve your taste, so that on the whole it would be safer and better to trust to drawings and photographs of really good works, which must be correct.

The carver will, doubtless, in many instances find it necessary to enlarge or increase the dimensions of his model or design, as it would be unlikely that he could find a drawing or photograph of precisely the requisite size. In this case we would advise him to adopt a mechanical plan in vogue amongst copyists, namely, to cover the face of the design with a network of horizontal and perpendicular lines by means of a light pencil or chalk; or if he does not wish to make marks on the design, stretch threads across from edge to edge in the following manner: the picture or photograph must first be fixed on a drawing board, or, if he has not one, any soft deal board which will not warp will do as well, then mark out a square enclosing it—let us say 12in. in size—of course, this will vary according to the dimensions of the photograph. Each inch on both sides and at the top and bottom must be exactly measured off and marked with a short steel pin or tack; strain threads first horizontally and then perpendicularly from pin to pin, then take a sheet of drawing paper of the exact size it is intended the carving to be, and on it rule the same number of lines as there are threads over the photograph. He will thus have the same number of squares in each, larger or smaller, as the case may be. In each square on the drawing paper sketch in the figure, part of figure, or whatever is the subject which is enclosed in the corresponding square of the photograph. By this simple method even the most clumsy draughtsman is enabled to make a sufficiently correct outline.

We have hitherto spoken of carving in basso relievo merely from a secular point of view, as works of art or embellishment

of a room.  But this style enters also largely into ecclesiastical
ornamentation, and there are few finer subjects for the carver's
skill than an altar piece, reredos, or panels of a like nature.
This, however, is not the place (nor, indeed, is it within the limit
we have given ourselves) to enter into details as regards this
special style of work.  Those of our readers who intend to turn
their attention to this branch of that art would do well before
they undertake any work of this kind to consult with an architect,
or someone well versed in such matters (unless he has studied
the subject himself), and to procure a slight sketch of the style
and proportions best suited to the church which he proposes to
decorate, in order that his work may amalgamate with the age and
architecture of the edifice.

As this book is intended purely as a guide to amateurs,
those designs have been chosen which we consider as especially
suited to this class, rather than to the professional carver,
and for this reason we have confined ourselves to drawings
and descriptions of such subjects as the amateur can execute
without the intervention of much professional help.

It will be obvious that it is quite impossible to become a good
carver from the information contained in any book.  It has been
stated before, and it is repeated here, that all that is attempted
in this little guide is to point the way.  More technical knowledge
will be gained in an hour or so of actual working under a trained
instructor than in many without such supervision.  The amateur
is therefore advised to attend a good School of Art; most towns
of any size possess one, and the instruction given is usually the
best of its kind obtainable.

Further, every opportunity should be taken to watch professional
men at work, and to obtain from them such useful tips as they will
sometimes give.  This must not be taken to suggest that the
worker should endeavour to emulate the practices of the carver of
cheap furniture, but rather should study the methods of those
engaged in first-class work, such as fittings for ecclesiastical and
official buildings.

Lastly, the character of the material must never be lost sight of or destroyed. Wood has characteristics which distinguish it from stone, plaster, or any other decorative medium, and these should be rigidly maintained in whatever ornament is employed. Let your carving always look as if it had been executed with tools and make no attempt to imitate a plaster cast.

r

# CHAPTER VIII.

## CHIP-CARVING.

LARGE numbers of amateurs are unable to take up a mechanical and artistic hobby either from the difficulty of learning, cost and number of tools, or from want of a special work-room. Those hindered by any of the above considerations cannot do better than take up chip-carving. Only one tool, purchasable for one shilling, is required; the work can be done in any ordinary room without causing a mess or litter; the art is easily acquired, and the physical labour slight. As chip-carving is by no means new as a recreation, no doubt many readers are aware that highly ornamental effects are to be got from it, and that the work, though simple, is extremely interesting. It is not, however, generally known how much may be done with the solitary tool above referred to. As a rule, the learner is told to use carving-tools of the ordinary kind. These are all very well in their way, but to use them properly requires a bench or table of some kind, and a fair amount of practice. Even when done with them, chip-carving as compared with ordinary carving is easy; but it is simpler still when done with the tool referred to. It is not a new one, but somehow or other it has escaped proper recognition

DESIGNS FOR CHIP CARVING.

of its powers. Those who have written on the subject of chip-carving have alluded to its existence, but as a rule that is all, although it is *the* tool for chip-carving, and easy though the work may be, a few directions will help the novice.

Perhaps, it will be well to explain what chip, or notch carving, as it is often called, is as distinguished from the ordinary kind. Briefly, it is a method of ornamenting surfaces generally, but not necessarily, flat, by cutting variously-shaped notches or hollows in them. These being arranged in an orderly manner, and mostly of a geometrical pattern, form the decoration. The cuts, it should be stated, are nearly always made on the slant from opposite directions, so that the bottom of each notch, instead of being flat, is merely the angle formed by the two sides. As we proceed further this will be more clearly seen ; in the meantime let the novice make with the point of a pen-knife two cuts, say ⅛in., or less apart, and of any length, through the surface of one piece of wood, and sloping downwards towards each other. Whatever the angle at which the cuts are made, they must meet. Now make two cuts at a similar slant at the ends of the long one, and a rectangular notch will be the result. This is the germ of all chip-carving, the pattern depending on the curve, size, and general arrangement of the notches.

FIG. 42.

The tool with which this carving may be done consists of a hooked blade fitted in a handle (as shown in Fig. 42), the blade being about 1½in. long. These knives are not generally kept at tool shops, but may be obtained from many dealers. In shape different blades vary slightly, as in Figs. 43 and 44, the former, being more rounded off and thinner towards the point, is to be preferred to the latter.

FIG. 43.

The carver does not require to support the work on a table or bench, though he may do so if desired. Generally it is just as easy to hold the wood in one hand and work the knife with the other. Instead, therefore, of having the work always lying flat on a table, it can be moved about to suit the kind of cut being made. Herein lies the great convenience of the knife compared with the ordinary carving-tools. To the majority of amateurs it will feel more familiar in the hand, from its resemblance to an ordinary knife. One way of holding it is with the handle firmly grasped in the right hand, and the first joint of the fore-finger curved over the back of the blade. This is specially useful when the wood is being held in the other hand, but unless the right hand is moved as the cut proceeds, does not give much freedom of action when the work is on a table. Another way of holding it, and one by which both power and freedom of action are gained, is to grasp the handle with all four fingers, not resting them on the work. The thumb gives the necessary support to afford steadiness to the cut, and allows of a cut of considerable length

FIG. 44.

being made. Great power may also be gained by resting the thumb against the edge of the piece of wood being carved, if this is not too large. The second and third methods will be found exceedingly useful when cutting curves, which are the most difficult notches at first.

In order to make a curved notch easily, the knife should be so held that the elbow is well away from the carver's body, so that the full sweep can be given with the blade.

Another method, requiring both hands, is to hold the knife in the right and press against the back of the blade with the left thumb. It is sometimes a relief to have recourse to this plan, especially when cutting straight lines, and it will be understood the work must be on some support.

These are all typical methods of making the cuts; but it must not be inferred that the knife may not be held in any other way. Any in which the carver finds he can get the most command over the tool will be the right way, and after a very small amount of practice no regard need be consciously paid to the way in which the knife is held; it will be held naturally in the best way to do the work intended.

As with other carving tools, the edge cannot be too sharp, so that no amount of trouble should be spared to get it into good condition and to keep it so. The carver should always work with a strop at hand, and give the blade a rub or two whenever its cutting powers show the smallest sign of giving way. An ordinary razor-strop does as well as anything, and it will not be long before the novice discerns the increased comfort to himself and benefit to the work of keeping the knife well stropped. To save him needless trouble, it may be well to say that nearly all the cutting is done with the $\frac{1}{2}$in. or so of edge nearest the point, so that the chief attention should be paid to this part. A blade with a back thick close up to the point is not as easy to cut with as one which is judiciously tapered.

With regard to the handle, all we would say about it is that though its polished condition when new may look very nice, the polish is rather an objection than otherwise. A firmer grip is got on an unpolished surface, and this will be found more noticeable when the hands are moist with perspiration. Mere good looks in this should give way to utility, and if desired the polish can easily be removed by scraping or with glass-paper. The novice may again be cautioned on no account to use glass-paper on the wood to smooth it before carving, or till the carving is finished ;

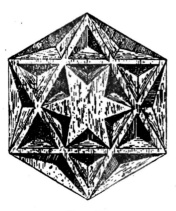

if he does, it will be found that the blade gets dull "in no time" from the small grits which have worked into the wood from the paper.

Although designs may very easily be made by the carver, it will be better to work, at first at any rate, from those which are to be had ready. A simple design, in which the notches are of a fair size and do not include too many small curves, should be chosen for the first attempt.

To anyone who can use a pair of compasses and a rule, or has any knowledge of practical geometry, the difficulty of drawing the designs on the wood will be so trifling as not to be worth considering. As the designs show the shading, and consequently the inner or bottom angles, and not merely the outlines on the surface, it will be well for the novice to know that he need only draw the latter ; the angles indicated by the others form themselves naturally as the cuts are

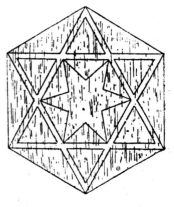

FIG. 46.

made. Thus Fig. 45 represents a regular hexagon, containing two triangles and a six-cornered star in the centre, as shown in the design. The lines at the bottoms of the shaded pockets, or notches, are clearly discernible, but need not be drawn on the wood ; on it merely the outline (as in Fig. 46) is required. An examination of Fig. 47 will clearly show how the various lines are set out, and, supposing the design is not transferred to the wood with carbon paper, fairly represents the drawing before carving is commenced.

In making the cuts, the precise angle at which the blade is inclined to the wood is not of much consequence, but it should be as uniform as possible. The hand will almost insensibly become accustomed to cutting at the same slope, or so nearly the same, that the difference in depth of the same sized notches in any piece of work is not notice-able. As far as possible, the cuts should be made cleanly and to the required depth at once. This, how-ever, is often impracticable, and it is necessary to make more than one cut to get to the bottom. When this has to be done, the utmost care should be taken that the second and succeeding cuts are exactly at the same angle as the first, for if not, the notch, or rather that parti-

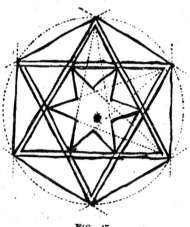

FIG. 47.

cular side of it, will show a ridge wherever the cut has been unequal, instead of being quite smooth. The irregularity may be pared away afterwards, but to do this is a waste of time, and the work seldom looks so clean as if done properly at first.

Perhaps the novice may be inclined to think that it would be easier to begin paring away a notch from the centre, gradually increasing the size till the outline is reached. At first it may be so ; but facility will not be obtained in doing the work, and he should begin, as indicated, boldly on the outline.

From the point of the knife penetrating further than it need at the bottom of the notches, it will often be observed that there is a kind of slight burr turned up. This may easily be removed if the work is small and for close inspection, otherwise it may be disregarded. The cuts themselves do not require any attention.

When the carving has been done, the work may be cleaned off with glass-paper used in the ordinary way over a cork block. It must be remembered that the notches themselves cannot be worked on with the paper, which only cleans up the surface of the wood. The dust will work itself into the cuts referred to in the previous paragraph, so that they will be barely distinguishable. To make the work as clean as possible it should be finally brushed with a stiff brush, and may then be regarded as complete.

As to the wood, very little need be said. At first it is not advisable to use any hard kind, and none is more suitable than a piece of good, sound, clean pine ; it is soft, and cuts cleanly. Another good kind to begin with is American white wood, though pine is on the whole to be preferred. In course of time it assumes a pleasant, warm tone. It or any other wood may be varnished, for French polishing is out of the question ; but it is a matter of opinion whether the appearance is improved, as size causes the surfaces to swell and roughen, and as there is no means of rubbing them down again it must not be used. The varnish must be applied instead till it does not sink. Stains are also objectionable for the same reasons as size. If any must be used, let them be mixed with spirits or turps instead of water, though even then the result is seldom pleasing, as more is absorbed by the end grain than elsewhere, giving the work a dirty, patchy look. A less objectionable way is to treat it with Aspinall's or some similar enamel. Instead of painting all over with one colour, the notches may be picked out with various tints, and if these are judiciously chosen very pleasing effects may be obtained. In the same way bronze paints of different tints may

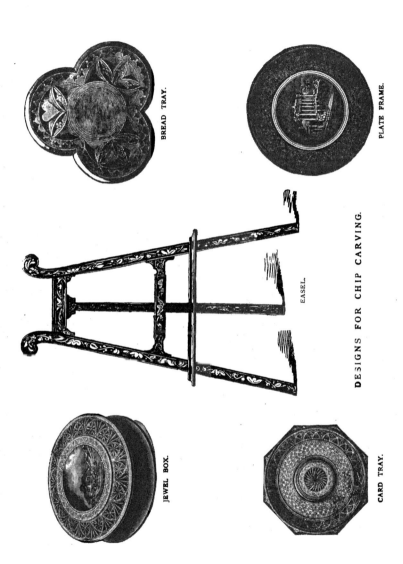

BREAD TRAY.

PLATE FRAME.

EASEL.

JEWEL BOX.

CARD TRAY.

DESIGNS FOR CHIP CARVING.

be used, though at some risk of the decoration tending rather to barbaric splendour than to artistic taste.

When sufficient progress has been made to enable it to be worked, there is no wood better than oak. Though hard, it is not unpleasant to cut if a nice piece has been got. It is not, however, suitable for very small work, for which a fine, close-grained wood should be chosen. Chip-carved oak looks remarkably well when darkened either by oiling or by fumigation, or by a combination of born, and then wax-polished. Varnish destroys its beauty, and gives it a coarse, commonplace appearance.

# CHAPTER IX.

## ORNAMENT AND ITS APPLICATION.

THE amateur, having acquired some measure of skill in the use of tools, will naturally seek to turn it to some account. He will be tempted to carve anything and everything, and it is in this connection that a word of warning must be given. If his carving is to be really and truly an art, he must be careful to do nothing that will make it otherwise. To do this he will have to learn the meaning and value of ornament.

A letter in a word or a word in a sentence, if in its proper place, has a definite value and meaning, but once it is misplaced it loses its significance and causes the word or sentence of which it is a part to become nonsense or to have its original meaning changed. It is equally true of Art. A piece of ornament, rightly used, has value in a decorative sense; but misapplied, it not only becomes meaningless but detracts from the appearance of whatever it is associated with. A piece of carving, however badly done, will be truer Art if rightly used than the most skilful example in the wrong place.

To acquire this very necessary knowledge involves much patient and earnest study of the styles of ornament, and the careful examination of good examples of old carving. It is quite beyond the scope of this book to go thoroughly into the history of the styles and periods, but the following brief notes may serve as an introduction to the subject.

Norman.

Early English.

Decorated.

Perpendicular.

FIG. 48.

From the coming of the Conqueror to the thirteenth century the architecture and decoration in vogue in this country were Romanesque or Norman. From this developed Gothic, which had three phases, the Early English, the Decorated, and the Perpendicular. The carving employed was in each case characteristic of the prevailing phase, as is shown in the examples (Fig. 48) given above.

During the sixteenth century the revival of Classic learning brought about the Renaissance. Classic forms and features were intermingled with those of Gothic origin, resulting in the Tudor and Jacobean styles. The carving associated with these is symbolic of the change of thought and the gradual spreading of knowledge which characterised the times. The spirit of Gothic is gradually displaced by that of Classic. As in Spenser's "Faerie Queene," Christian and pagan signs and personalities are introduced in a strange medley. What the craftsman lacked in knowledge

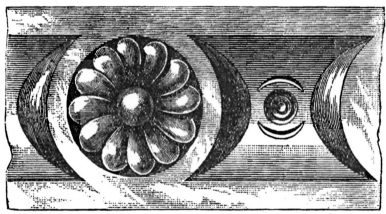

FIG. 49.

of Classic design he made up for with his imagination and fancy, and to this is traceable the great variety of ornament and decoration which is found in the work of this period. The examples shown (Figs. 49, 50 and 51) are fairly typical of these styles.

The pure English Renaissance style did not develop till the seventeenth century, and in many cases the ornament adopted was based on the acanthus and bayleaf as in Classic times, but many other types of foliage and other objects are to be found reproduced in the work of the period. Under Grinling Gibbons' carving reached its highest degree of perfection.

A few characteristic examples (Figs. 52, 53 and 54) are given, and if they are compared with those of the Gothic style on p. 75, the change of " spirit " will be seen.

FIG. 50.

The study of actual work may be made in a local museum, in old parish or city churches, and in a multitude of ways available to most people. Attention should be paid to the position occupied by the carving, to its harmony and contrast to its surroundings,

Fig. 51.

to the fact of its subordination to the utilitarian and structural part of the example. It is these manifestations of restraint and reason which make for charm, and it is the lack of them which ruin so much amateur work. Who has not been asked to admire a

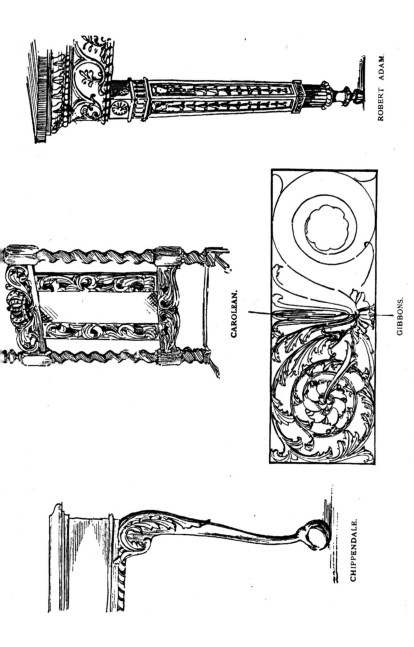

ROBERT ADAM.

CAROLEAN.

GIBBONS.

CHIPPENDALE.

EXAMPLES OF SEVENTEENTH AND EIGHTEENTH CENTURY CARVING.

table with even the top, which reason suggests should be smooth, covered with ornament ?  Such a thing can never be a joy for ever, but rather an eyesore for all beholders.

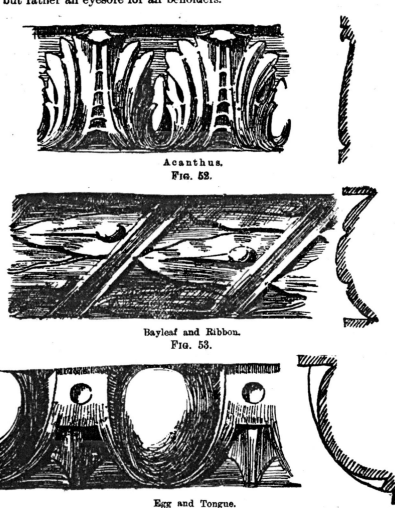

Acanthus.
Fig. 52.

Bayleaf and Ribbon.
Fig. 53.

Egg and Tongue.
Fig. 54.

A slavish imitation of old work is not by any means suggested, but rather the application of the principles which governed its execution.

Originality in conformity with the precepts of Art is to be aimed at, and in this connection, although the power of design depends upon the talent possessed, much can be effected if it is borne in mind that design is the opposite to haphazard.

Flowers, fruit, or anything else that appeals to the individual taste may be used, the objects should be carefully studied and the knowledge gained applied in design, always remembering that it is not a portrait that is required, but a decorative treatment of the panel or whatsoever else it may happen to be.

In this way will the amateur be able to exercise his fancy and imagination, and this, combined with the regard for the principles of ornament which will come as a result of knowledge, will help him to produce something worthy of the name of the art of carving.

# INDEX.

## A.

Acanthus ornament, 79
Advantages of the art, 1
American white wood, 18
Apple wood, 14, 15
Appliances, 19

## B.

Basso-relievo carving, 61
   Subjects for, 61
Bayleaf and ribbon ornament, 79
Bench holdfast, for flat work, 23
   Vice, 22
Bent tools, 8
Birds, Suitability of, for design, 55
Book-slide, 53
Boxwood, 14, 15
Brucciani and Co., 63
Bureau, Carved, facing p. 34

## C.

Carpenter's bench, 19
Carpentry and wood-carving compared, 3
   As an aid to wood-carving, 2

Carving, 17th and 18th Century, facing p. 78
Chip-carving, 66
   Designs, 70, and facing pp. 10, 53, 66, and 72
   Distinguishing features of, 67
   Enamelling, 72
   Holding the work, 68
   Oak, 73
   Stropping the tool, 69
   Tool, 66, 67
   Varnishing, 72
   Woods, 72
Chisels, Corner, 7
   Skew, 7
Clay, Modelling in, 55
Curved tools, 8
Cutting tools, Sharpening, 32
Cypress wood, 14

## D.

Decorated style, 75
Decorative carving, Simple design for, 39
Defective wood, 15
Designs, Frontispiece.
   Book-slide, 53
   Chip-carving, 70

G

82    INDEX.

Designs, Fret-cutting, 50
 Geometric, 39
 Grotesque, 39
 Grounding-out, 50
 Lectern, 57
 Panel-carving. *See* Frontis-
  piece and 34
 Paper-knife handle, 43, 48
 Rustic panel, 48
Device for attaching to panels,
  26, 27
Drill, 45

**E.**

Eagle design for lectern, 57
Early English style, 75
Ebony, 14, 15
 Liability to crack, 15
 Varieties of, 16
Ecclesiastical carvings, 64
Edges of tools, Form of, 29
Egg and tongue ornament, 79
Enamelling chip-carving, 72
Examples for carving, 43

**F.**

" Feeling," 2
Fig-wood, 14
Files, Bent, 13
Finishing-off work, 42
Flaws in wood, 15
Fret-cutting a design, 50
Fret-sawing, 50

**G.**

Geometric design, 39
Gibbons, Grinling, 15, 76
Gilding, 52
 Materials, 52
 Preparing the work, 52
 Tools, 52

Glass-paper, Use of, deprecated,
  42
Gothic carving, facing p. 43
Gouges, Bent-back, 8
 Flat, 6
 Sharpening, 30
 Sweep of, 7
Grinding tools, 28
Grotesque design, 39
Grounding-out a design, 50

**H.**

Handles, Tool, 9
 Ready-made, 9
Handscrew, 24
Hardwoods, 15
Holding tools, 41
 Wood, 22
Holly, 14, 15
Horse-chestnut, 14

**I.**

Improving an oilstone, 12

**L.**

Lemon wood, 14
Levelling ground for relief-
  carving, 11
Lime, 14, 15

**M.**

Mahogany, 14
 Honduras, 15
 Spanish, 15
 Varieties of, 14
Makeshifts, 2
Mallet, 10
Materials for gilding, 52
Misapplied ornament, 75
Modelling in clay, 55

## N.

Nail as punch substitute, 12
Norman style, 75
Notch carving, 67

## O.

Oak, 14, 73
Oilstone, 12
Ordering wood, 17
Ornament and its application, 75
Outline for panel-carving, 35

## P.

Panel-carving, 34
    Conventional treatment necessary, 35
    Cutting the design, 35
    Designs for. *See* Frontispiece and 34
    Drawing the outline, 35
    Making the design, 34
    Method of cutting, 35
    Punching the ground, 38
    Treatment of relief portion, 38
    Trimming away waste wood, 36, 38
    Undercutting, 38
    Woods for, 35
Paper-knife handle, 43, 48
Parting-tool, 7
Pear wood, 15
Perpendicular style, 75
Pine wood, 17
Plane, 14
"Plant," 2
Plasticine, 36
Punch, Form of, 12
    French nail as substitute, 12
Punching the ground of a carving, 38

## R.

Relief-carving, Levelling ground for, 11
Renaissance, The, 76
Rifflers, 12
Roughness in tools, Rubbing down, 30
Router, 11
Rustic frame, Treatment of, 48

## S.

Sandal wood, 14
Screw, Wood-carver's, 23
Seasoning wood, 17
Sets of tools, 9
"Shakes" in woods, 15
Sharpening tools, 28, 33
Spanish chestnut, 14
Spanish mahogany, 15
Straight tools, 8
Stropping tools, 13, 32, 69
Subjects for basso-relievo carving, 61
Sycamore wood, 15

## T.

Table for working on, 19, 20, 21
Table-top, Method of protecting, 24
Testing tools for sharpness, 33
Tool-handles, 9
    Shape, 9
    Wood for, 9
Tools, 5
    Bench holdfast, 23
    Bench-vice, 22
    Bent, 8, 12
    Chip-carving, 66, 67
    Corner chisels, 7
    Curved, 8
    Drill, 45

Tools, Edges of, 29
   Flat gouges, 6
   Gilding, 52
   Grinding, 28
   Hand-screw, 24
   Holding, 35, 41
   Mallet, 10
   Number of, 6
   Oilstone, 12
   Parting-tool, 7
   Punch, 12
   Ready-made, 9
   Rifflers, 12
   Router, 11
   Rubbing down roughness, 30
   Selecting, 6, 8
   Sets, 5, 9
   Sharpening, 28, 33
   Skew chisels, 7
   Straight, 8
   Stropping, 13, 32
   Testing for sharpness, 33
   Wood-carver's screw, 23
Treatment of chip-carved oak, 73
Trimming the work, 36, 38

U.

Undercutting, 38

V.

Varnishing chip-carving, 72
Vine, Treatment of, 38
V-tool, 7
   Sharpening. 31

W.

Walnut, 14
Woods, American white, 18
   Apple, 14, 15
   Box, 14, 15
   Characteristics of, 66
   Chip-carving, 72
   Choice of, 14
   Cypress, 14
   Defects, 15
   Ebony, 14, 15
   Fig, 14
   Flaws in, 15
   For panel-carving, 35
   Hard, 15
   Holly, 14, 15
   Horse-chestnut, 14
   Lemon, 14
   Lime, 14, 15
   Mahogany, 14, 15
   Method of selling, 15
   Oak, 14, 73
   Ordering, 17
   Pear, 15
   Pine, 17
   Plane. 14
   Sandal, 14
   Seasoning, 17
   " Shakes " in, 15
   Spanish chestnut, 14
   Spanish mahogany, 15
   Sycamore, 15
   Walnut, 14
Workshop, 19
Work-table, 19, 20. 21

Lightning Source UK Ltd.
Milton Keynes UK
171404UK00001B/6/P